This Book Belongs To

_____

_____

© Copyright 2021 - All rights reserved.

You may not reproduce, duplicate or send the contents of this book without direct written permission from the author. You cannot hereby despite any circumstance blame the publisher or hold him or her to legal responsibility for any reparation, compensations, or monetary forfeiture owing to the information included herein, either in a direct or an indirect way.
Legal Notice: This book has copyright protection. You can use the book for personal purpose. You should not sell, use, alter, distribute, quote, take excerpts or paraphrase in part or whole the material contained in this book without obtaining the permission of the author first.
Disclaimer Notice: You must take note that the information in this document is for casual reading and entertainment purposes only.

Contents

Festive Appetizers & Beverages — 7
Beef Canapes with Cucumber Sauce — 8
Hot Buttered Rum Mix — 9
Bacon-Cheese Biscuit Bites — 10
Calzone Pinwheels — 11
Cranberry Chili Meatballs — 12
Mushroom Cheese Bread — 13
Layered Shrimp Dip — 14
Mini Chimichangas — 15
Tomato Pizza Bread — 16
Pomegranate Martini — 17

Holiday Parties — 18
Grilled Cheese Supreme — 19
Roasted Red Pepper Bisque — 20
Spinach Festival Salad — 21
Mushroom Tartlets — 22
Baked Crab Rangoon — 23
Grape Juice Sparkler — 24
Roast Beef and Pear Crostini — 25
Layered Blue Cheese Spread — 26
Apricot Chicken Wings — 27
Cranberry Tea — 28

Joyful Brunches — 29

Contents

Southwestern Omele 30
Overnight Raisin French Toast 31
Citrus Cooler 32
Egg Scramble 33
Vanilla Fruit Salad 34
Colorful Brunch Frittata 35
Hot Fruit Compote 36
Sage Breakfast Patties 37
Gingerbread Pancakes 38
Cinnamon Peach Kuchen 39

Christmas Dinner Menu 40

Peppercorn Beef Top Loin Roast 41
Garlic Baby Potatoes 42
Jarlsberg Popovers 43
Zesty Broccolini 44
Coconut Cranberry Shortcakes 45
Apple Cider-Glazed Ham 46
Merry Berry Salad 47
Dijon Green Beans 48
Bacon Caesar Salad 49
Baked Sweet Onions 50

Merry Entrees 51

Cherry-Stuffed Pork Chops 52

Contents

Seafood en Croute 53
Baked Lobster Tails 54
Spinach Steak Pinwheels 55
Spiral Ham with Cranberry Glaze 56
Garlic Pork Roast 57
Duck with Cherry Sauce 58
Baked Ham with Orange Glaze 59
Pesto Pepper Tortellini 60
Champagne Baked Ham 61

Jolly Sides 62

Company's Coming Salad 63
Beans with Parsley Sauce 64
Gingered Orange Beets 65
Spinach Almond Salad 66
Black-Eyed Peas with Bacon 67
Cranberry Gelatin Mold 68
Marinated Italian Salad 69
Peas in Cheese Sauce 70
Baked Rice Pilaf 71
Balsamic-Glazed Brussels Sprouts 72

Glorious Breads 73

Merry Christmas Scones 74
Multigrain Bread 75

Contents

Cracked Pepper Cheddar Muffins — 76
Grandma's Honey Muffins — 77
Mini Toffee Rolls — 78
Apple Spice Muffins — 79
Cheddar Garlic Biscuits — 80
Sweet Potato Biscuits — 81
Lemony Poppy Seed Muffins — 82
Sweet Potato Rolls — 83

Yuletide Cookies & Bars — 84

Orange-Cinnamon Chocolate Chip Cookies — 85
Coconut Crunch Cookies — 86
Snickerdoodles — 87
Decorated Christmas Cutout Cookies — 88
Slice 'n' Bake Fruitcake Cookies — 89
Polka-Dot Macaroons — 90
Cherry Kisses — 91
Peppermint Meltaways — 92
Date Nut Icebox Cookies — 93
Gingerbread Cookies — 94

Heavenly Desserts — 95

Pumpkin Pound Cake — 96
Peppermint Puff Pastry Sticks — 97
Apple Pie in a Goblet — 98

Contents

Maple-Mocha Brownie Torte	99
Snowflake Pudding	100
Coconut Angel Squares	101
Pomegranate Poached Pears	102
Berries with Champagne Cream	103
Raspberry Fondue Dip	104
Steamed Cranberry-Molasses Pudding	105
Candy Sampler	106
Chocolate-Coated Pretzels	107
Cookie Dough Truffles	108
Butterscotch Fudge	109
Raisin Cashew Drops	110
So-Easy Truffles	111
Snowball	112
Cinnamon Walnut Brittle	113
Toasted Coconut Truffles	114
Holiday Divinity	115
Peanut Butter Chocolate Cups	116
Thank you page	118

Festive Appetizers & Beverages

Beef Canapes with Cucumber Sauce

PREP: 30 MIN. + CHILLING BAKE: 25 MIN. + CHILLING MAKES: 3 DOZEN

Ingredients

4 cups (32 ounces) plain yogurt - 1 beef tenderloin roast (1 1/2 pounds) - 2 tablespoons olive oil, divided - 1 teaspoon salt, divided - 1/4 teaspoon plus 1/8 teaspoon white pepper, divided - 1 medium cucumber, peeled, seeded and diced - 1 tablespoon finely chopped onion - 1 garlic clove, minced - 1 tablespoon white vinegar - 1 French bread baguette (1 pound), cut into 36 thin slices - 1 cup fresh arugula Sliced grape tomatoes, optional

1. Line a fine mesh strainer with two layers of cheesecloth; place over a bowl. Place yogurt in strainer. Cover and refrigerate for at least 4 hours or overnight.
2. Rub tenderloin with 1 tablespoon oil. Sprinkle with 1/2 teaspoon salt and 1/4 teaspoon white pepper. In a large skillet, cook tenderloin over medium-high heat until browned on all sides. Transfer to a shallow roasting pan.
3. Bake at 400° for 25-30 minutes or until a thermometer reads 145°. Cool on a wire rack for 1 hour. Cover and refrigerate.
4. Transfer yogurt from strainer to another bowl (discard yogurt liquid). Add the cucumber, onion, garlic and remaining salt and white pepper. In a small bowl, whisk the vinegar and remaining oil; stir into yogurt mixture.
5. Thinly slice the tenderloin. Spread yogurt mixture over bread slices; top with beef, arugula and, if desired, tomato slices. Serve immediately or cover and refrigerate until serving.

Hot Buttered Rum Mix

PREP: 10 MIN. + FREEZING MAKES: 14-18 SERVINGS

Ingredients

1 cup butter, softened • 2 cups confectioners' sugar • 1 cup plus 2 tablespoons packed brown sugar • 2 cups vanilla ice cream, softened • 1 1/2 teaspoons ground cinnamon • 1/2 teaspoon ground nutmeg • 1 teaspoon rum extract

ADDITIONAL INGREDIENT (FOR EACH SERVING)

3/4 cup boiling water

In a large bowl, cream butter and sugars until light and fluffy. Add the ice cream, cinnamon, nutmeg and extract. Transfer to a freezer container; freeze overnight. Yield: 3 1/2 cups mix.

To prepare hot drink: *Dissolve 3-4 tablespoons of mix in boiling water; stir well.*

Bacon-Cheese Biscuit Bites

PREP: 20 MIN. BAKE: 15 MIN. MAKES: 20 APPETIZERS

Ingredients

4 ounces cream cheese, softened - 1 egg - 1 tablespoon 2% milk - 1/3 cup real bacon bits - 1/4 cup shredded Swiss cheese - 1 tablespoon dried minced onion - 1 large plum tomato, seeded and finely chopped, divided - 1 tube (10.2 ounces) large refrigerated flaky biscuits

1. In a small bowl, beat the cream cheese, egg and milk until smooth. Stir in the bacon, cheese, onion and half of the tomato; set aside.
2. Cut each biscuit into four pieces; press each piece into a greased miniature muffin cup. Fill with cream cheese mixture; top with remaining tomato.
3. Bake at 375° for 14-16 minutes or until a knife inserted near the center comes out clean.

Calzone Pinwheels

PREP/TOTAL TIME: 30 MIN. MAKES: 16 APPETIZERS

Ingredients

1/2 cup ricotta cheese; 1 teaspoon Italian seasoning; 1/4 teaspoon salt;
1/2 cup shredded part-skim mozzarella cheese 1/2 cup diced pepperoni;
1/4 cup grated Parmesan cheese; 1/4 cup chopped fresh mushrooms; 1/4 cup finely chopped green pepper; 2 tablespoons finely chopped onion;
1 package (8 ounces) refrigerated crescent rolls 1 jar (14 ounces) pizza sauce, warmed;

1. In a small bowl, combine the ricotta, Italian seasoning and salt. Stir in the mozzarella cheese, pepperoni, Parmesan cheese, mushrooms, green pepper and onion. Separate crescent dough into four rectangles; seal perforations.
2. Spread cheese mixture over each rectangle to within 1/4 in. of edges. Roll up jelly-roll style, starting with a short side; pinch seams to seal. Cut each into four slices.
3. Place cut side down on greased baking sheets. Bake at 375° for 10-15 minutes or until golden brown. Serve warm with pizza sauce. Refrigerate leftovers.

Cranberry Chili Meatballs

PREP/TOTAL TIME: 30 MIN. MAKES: ABOUT 6 DOZEN

Ingredients

1 can (14 ounces) jellied cranberry sauce 1 bottle (12 ounces) chili sauce
3/4 cup packed brown sugar
1/2 teaspoon chili powder
1/2 teaspoon ground cumin
1/4 teaspoon cayenne pepper
1 package (32 ounces) frozen fully cooked homestyle meatballs, thawed

In a large saucepan over medium heat, combine the first six ingredients; stir until sugar is dissolved. Add meatballs; cook for 20-25 minutes or until heated through, stirring occasionally.

Mushroom Cheese Bread

PREP: 25 MIN. BAKE: 20 MIN. MAKES: 16 SERVINGS

Ingredients

6 cups sliced fresh mushrooms
1 tablespoon butter
4 green onions, chopped
1 loaf (1 pound) French bread
1 carton (8 ounces) spreadable garlic and herb cream cheese 2 cups (8 ounces) shredded Italian cheese blend
1 cup mayonnaise
1 cup grated Parmesan cheese

1. In a large skillet, saute the mushrooms in butter until tender. Add onions; cook and stir until liquid has evaporated. Set aside.
2. Cut French bread in half lengthwise and then widthwise; spread cut sides with cream cheese. Combine the Italian cheese, mayonnaise and Parmesan cheese; spread over bread. Top with mushroom mixture.
3. Place on a baking sheet. Bake at 350° for 20 minutes or until cheese is melted. If desired, broil 4-6 in. from the heat for 2-4 minutes or until golden brown. Slice and serve warm.

Layered Shrimp Dip

PREP: 15 MIN. + CHILLING MAKES: 12-16 SERVINGS

Ingredients

1 package (3 ounces) cream cheese, softened
6 tablespoons salsa, divided
1/2 cup cocktail sauce
3 cans (6 ounces each) small shrimp, rinsed and drained 1 can (21/4 ounces) sliced ripe olives, drained
1 cup (4 ounces) shredded cheddar cheese
1 cup (4 ounces) shredded Monterey Jack cheese
Sliced green onions
Tortilla chips

1. In a small bowl, combine cream cheese and 3 tablespoons salsa; spread into an ungreased 9-in. pie plate. Combine cocktail sauce and remaining salsa; spread over cream cheese.

2. Arrange shrimp evenly over top. Sprinkle with olives. Combine cheeses; sprinkle over top. Add onions. Chill. Serve with tortilla chips.

Mini Chimichangas

PREP: 1 HOUR COOK: 15 MIN. MAKES: 14 SERVINGS

Ingredients

1 pound ground beef; 1 medium onion, chopped; 1 envelope taco seasoning; 3/4 cup water; 3 cups (12 ounces) shredded Monterey Jack cheese; 1 cup (8 ounces) sour cream; 1 can (4 ounces) chopped green chilies, drained; 1 package (1 pound) egg roll wrappers (14 count); 1 egg white, lightly beaten
Oil for deep-fat frying; Salsa and additional sour cream

1. In a large skillet, cook beef and onion over medium heat until meat is no longer pink; drain. Stir in taco seasoning and water. Bring to a boil. Reduce heat; simmer, uncovered, for 5 minutes, stirring occasionally. Remove from the heat; cool slightly.
2. In a large bowl, combine the cheese, sour cream and chilies. Stir in beef mixture. Place an egg roll wrapper on work surface with one point facing you. Place 1/3 cup filling in center. Fold bottom third of wrapper over filling; fold in sides.
3. Brush top point with egg white; roll up to seal. Repeat with remaining wrappers and filling. (Keep remaining egg roll wrappers covered with waxed paper to avoid drying out.)
4. In a large saucepan, heat 1 in. of oil to 375°. Fry chimichangas for 11/2 minutes on each side or until golden brown. Drain on paper towels. Serve warm with salsa and sour cream.

Tomato Pizza Bread

PREP/TOTAL TIME: 30 MIN. MAKES: 8 SERVINGS

Ingredients

1 tube (13.8 ounces) refrigerated pizza crust
2 garlic cloves, minced
1/2 teaspoon dried oregano
1 cup (4 ounces) shredded part-skim mozzarella cheese, divided
1 plum tomato, halved lengthwise and thinly sliced
1/2 teaspoon Italian seasoning, optional

1. On a greased baking sheet, roll pizza crust into a 12-in. x 8-in. rectangle. Bake at 425° for 6-8 minutes or until the edges are lightly browned. Sprinkle with garlic, oregano and half of the cheese.
2. Arrange tomato slices in a single layer over cheese. Top with remaining cheese and, if desired, Italian seasoning. Bake 6-8 minutes longer or until cheese is melted and crust is lightly browned.

Pomegranate Martini

PREP/TOTAL TIME: 5 MIN. MAKES: 1 SERVING

Ingredients

Ice cubes
2 ounces pomegranate juice 1 ounce vodka
1/2 ounce triple sec
1/2 ounce club soda
1/2 teaspoon lemon juice
GARNISH
Pomegranate seeds

Fill a shaker three-fourths full with ice. Add the pomegranate juice, vodka, triple sec, club soda and lemon juice. Cover and shake for 10-15 seconds or until condensation forms on outside of shaker.
Strain into a chilled cocktail glass. Garnish as desired.

Holiday Parties

Grilled Cheese Supreme

PREP/TOTAL TIME: 20 MIN. MAKES: 6 SERVINGS

Ingredients

12 slices hearty rye bread
12 teaspoons mayonnaise
18 slices cheddar cheese
3 small tomatoes, thinly sliced 11/2 cups sliced fresh mushrooms 6 thin slices sweet onion
1 medium ripe avocado, peeled and cut into 12 wedges 12 teaspoons butter, softened

1. Spread each of six slices of bread with 1 teaspoon mayonnaise; layer with a cheese slice, tomato slices, mushrooms, another cheese slice, onion, 2 avocado wedges and remaining cheese slice. Spread remaining bread with remaining mayonnaise; place on top.
2. Butter outsides of sandwiches. Toast on a heated griddle for 2-3 minutes on each side or until bread is lightly browned and cheese is melted.

Roasted Red Pepper Bisque

PREP: 30 MIN. + STANDING COOK: 20 MIN. MAKES: 6 SERVINGS (2 QUARTS)

Ingredients

8 medium sweet red peppers 1 large onion, chopped
2 tablespoons butter
3 cups chicken broth, divided 2 cups half-and-half cream 1/2 teaspoon salt
1/2 teaspoon white pepper
6 tablespoons shredded Parmesan cheese

1. Broil peppers 4 in. from the heat until skins blister, about 5 minutes. With tongs, rotate peppers a quarter turn. Broil and rotate until all sides are blistered and blackened. Immediately place peppers in a large bowl; cover and let stand for 15-20 minutes.
2. Peel off and discard charred skin. Remove stems and seeds; set peppers aside.
3. In a large saucepan, saute onion in butter until tender; cool slightly. In a blender, combine the onion mixture, 2 cups broth and roasted peppers; cover and process until smooth. Return to the pan.
4. Stir in cream and remaining broth; heat through (do not boil). Stir in salt and pepper. Sprinkle each serving with 1 tablespoon cheese.

Spinach Festival Salad

PREP: 30 MIN. + STANDING MAKES: 6 SERVINGS

Ingredients

1 medium sweet yellow pepper; 1 medium sweet red pepper; 1/2 pound sliced deli turkey, cut into strips; 1 package (6 ounces) fresh baby spinach; 2 plum tomatoes, sliced; 2 green onions, sliced; 1/2 cup crumbled tomato and basil feta cheese; 3 pepperoncini, sliced; 2 tablespoons grated Romano cheese; 1 to 2 garlic cloves, minced; 1 teaspoon Italian seasoning; 1/2 teaspoon crushed red pepper flakes; 1/2 teaspoon pepper; 3/4 cup balsamic vinaigrette

1. Broil peppers 4 in. from the heat until skins blister, about 5 minutes. With tongs, rotate peppers a quarter turn. Broil and rotate until all sides are blistered and blackened. Immediately place peppers in a bowl; cover and let stand for 15-20 minutes.
2. Meanwhile, in a salad bowl, combine the turkey, spinach, tomatoes, onions, feta cheese, pepperoncini, Romano cheese, garlic and seasonings.
3. Peel off and discard charred skin from peppers. Remove stems and seeds. Slice peppers; add to salad and toss to combine. Serve with vinaigrette.

Mushroom Tartlets

PREP: 20 MIN. + CHILLING BAKE: 15 MIN. MAKES: ABOUT 3 DOZEN

Ingredients

1 package (8 ounces) cream cheese, softened 1/2 cup butter, softened
1 1/2 cups all-purpose flour
FILLING
1 pound fresh mushrooms, finely chopped 2 tablespoons butter
1 package (3 ounces) cream cheese, cubed 1/2 teaspoon salt
1/4 teaspoon dried thyme

1. In a small bowl, beat cream cheese and butter until light and fluffy. Add flour; beat until mixture forms a ball. Cover and refrigerate for 1 hour.
2. For filling, in a large skillet, saute mushrooms in butter. Drain and pat dry. Return to the pan; stir in cream cheese until melted. Stir in salt and thyme; set aside.
3. On a lightly floured surface, roll dough to 1/16-in. thickness; cut into 2 1/2-in. circles. Press onto the bottoms and up the sides of greased miniature muffin cups. Place a rounded teaspoonful of filling in each cup.
4. Bake at 350° for 12-17 minutes or until edges are lightly browned. Remove from pans to wire racks. Serve warm.

Baked Crab Rangoon

PREP/TOTAL TIME: 30 MIN. MAKES: 1 DOZEN

Ingredients

12 wonton wrappers
4 ounces cream cheese, softened
1/4 cup mayonnaise
1 can (6 ounces) crabmeat, drained, flaked and cartilage removed 1/4 cup thinly sliced green onions

1. Press wonton wrappers into greased miniature muffin cups. Bake at 350° for 6-7 minutes or until lightly browned.
2. Meanwhile, in a small bowl, beat cream cheese and mayonnaise until smooth. Stir in crab and onions; spoon into wonton cups. Bake for 10-12 minutes or until heated through. Serve warm.

Grape Juice Sparkler

PREP/TOTAL TIME: 15 MIN. MAKES: 10 SERVINGS (2 QUARTS)

Ingredients

1 can (11 1/2 ounces) frozen cranberry-raspberry juice concentrate, thawed
1 bottle (1 liter) club soda, chilled
1 bottle (750 ml) sparkling white grape juice, chilled
20 to 30 fresh raspberries

Just before serving, combine juice concentrate with club soda in a large pitcher. Stir in sparkling grape juice. Place two to three raspberries in the bottom of each glass; add juice.

Editor's Note: *Use 2 cans of cranberry-raspberry juice concentrate and 2 teaspoons lemon juice for a sweeter, fruitier beverage.*

Roast Beef and Pear Crostini

PREP/TOTAL TIME: 30 MIN. MAKES: 40 APPETIZERS

Ingredients

1 French bread baguette (1 pound) 3 tablespoons olive oil
1 garlic clove, minced
1 cup blue cheese salad dressing
1 medium pear, diced
1/4 cup thinly sliced green onions
2 cups cubed cooked roast beef
1 cup diced seeded tomatoes
1/2 teaspoon salt
1/4 teaspoon pepper
1/2 cup fresh basil leaves, thinly sliced

1. Cut the baguette into 40 slices. Combine oil and garlic; brush over one side of each slice of bread. Place on an ungreased baking sheet. Bake at 350° for 6-9 minutes or until lightly toasted.
2. Combine the salad dressing, pear and onions. Combine the roast beef, tomatoes, salt and pepper. Spread dressing mixture over toasted bread; top with beef mixture and basil.

Layered Blue Cheese Spread

PREP/TOTAL TIME: 25 MIN. MAKES: 4 CUPS

Ingredients

3 packages (8 ounces each) cream cheese, softened, divided
1 cup (4 ounces) crumbled blue cheese
1/4 cup plus 1 tablespoon sour cream, divided
2 tablespoons minced fresh parsley
1 tablespoon minced fresh cilantro
1 tablespoon minced chives
1/2 teaspoon coarsely ground pepper
1/2 cup chopped walnuts
Assorted breads or crackers

1. On a serving plate, spread two packages of cream cheese into an 8-in. circle. In a small bowl, combine the blue cheese, 1/4 cup sour cream, parsley, cilantro, chives and pepper until blended. Spread over cream cheese layer to within 1/2 in. of the edges.

2. In a small bowl, beat remaining cream cheese and sour cream until smooth. Spread over blue cheese layer to within 1 in. of the edges. Sprinkle with walnuts just before serving. Serve with breads or crackers.

Apricot Chicken Wings

PREP: 15 MIN. + MARINATING BAKE: 30 MIN. MAKES: 2 DOZEN

Ingredients

2 pounds chicken wings
1 cup apricot preserves
2 tablespoons cider vinegar
2 teaspoons hot pepper sauce
1 teaspoon chili powder
1 garlic clove, minced

1. Cut chicken wings into three sections; discard wing tips. In a small bowl, combine the remaining ingredients; pour 1/2 cup into a large resealable plastic bag. Add chicken; seal bag and turn to coat. Refrigerate for 4 hours or overnight. Cover and refrigerate remaining marinade.
2. Drain wings and discard marinade. Place wings in a greased foil-lined 15-in. x 10-in. x 1-in. baking pan. Bake at 400° for 30-35 minutes or until juices run clear, turning and basting occasionally with remaining marinade.
Editor's Note: *Uncooked chicken wing sections (wingettes) may be substituted for whole chicken wings.*

Cranberry Tea

PREP/TOTAL TIME: 30 MIN. MAKES: 3 QUARTS

Ingredients

3 cinnamon sticks (3 inches)
6 whole cloves
6 cups water
3 cups fresh or frozen cranberries
9 slices peeled fresh gingerroot
6 individual tea bags
6 cups unsweetened apple juice 1/3 cup honey

1. Place cinnamon and cloves on a double thickness of cheesecloth. Bring up corners of cloth; tie with a string to form a bag.
2. In a large saucepan, combine the water, cranberries and ginger; add spice bag. Bring to a boil. Reduce heat; cover and simmer for 15-20 minutes or until berries have popped, stirring occasionally. Remove from the heat. Add tea bags; cover and steep for 5 minutes.
3. Discard tea bags and spice bag. Strain cranberry mixture through a cheesecloth-lined colander. Return to saucepan. Stir in juice and honey; heat through. Serve warm.

Joyful Brunches

Southwestern Omelet

PREP/TOTAL TIME: 20 MIN. MAKES: 4 SERVINGS

Ingredients

1/2 cup chopped onion
1 jalapeno pepper, minced
1 tablespoon canola oil
6 egg, lightly beaten
6 bacon strips, cooked and crumbled
1 small tomato, chopped
1 ripe avocado, cut into 1-inch slices
1 cup (4 ounces) shredded Monterey Jack cheese, divided
Salt and pepper to taste
Salsa, optional

1. In a large skillet, saute onion and jalapeno in oil until tender; remove with a slotted spoon and set aside. Pour eggs into the same skillet; cover and cook over low heat for 3-4 minutes.

2. Sprinkle with the onion mixture, bacon, tomato, avocado and 1/2 cup cheese. Season with salt and pepper.

3. Fold omelet in half over filling. Cover and cook for 3-4 minutes or until eggs are set. Sprinkle with remaining cheese. Serve with salsa if desired.

Editor's Note: *Wear disposable gloves when cutting hot peppers; the oils can burn skin. Avoid touching your face.*

Overnight Raisin French Toast

PREP: 15 MIN. + CHILLING BAKE: 45 MIN. MAKES: 12 SERVINGS

Ingredients

1 loaf (1 pound) cinnamon-raisin bread, cubed
1 package (8 ounces) cream cheese, cubed
8 eggs, lightly beaten
1 1/2 cups half-and-half cream
1/2 cup sugar
1/2 cup maple syrup
2 tablespoons vanilla extract 1 tablespoon ground cinnamon
1/8 teaspoon ground nutmeg

1. Place half of the bread cubes in a greased 13-in. x 9-in. baking dish. Top with cream cheese and remaining bread.
2. In a large bowl, whisk the remaining ingredients. Pour over top. Cover and refrigerate overnight.
3. Remove from the refrigerator 30 minutes before baking. Cover and bake at 350° for 30 minutes. Uncover; bake 15-20 minutes longer or until a knife inserted near the center comes out clean.

Citrus Cooler

PREP/TOTAL TIME: 5 MIN. MAKES: 2 SERVINGS

Ingredients

1/2 cup grapefruit juice
1/2 cup orange juice
1 to 2 teaspoons lime juice
1 cup ginger ale, chilled
8 ice cubes
Lime and orange slices, optional

In a large bowl, combine the grapefruit juice, orange juice, lime juice and ginger ale. Serve in two chilled glasses over ice. Garnish with lime and orange slices if desired.

Egg Scramble

PREP: 15 MIN. COOK: 20 MIN. MAKES: 10 SERVINGS

Ingredients

1 1/2 cups diced peeled potatoes; 1/2 cup chopped sweet red pepper; 1/2 cup chopped green pepper; 1/2 cup chopped onion
2 teaspoons canola oil, divided; 2 cups cubed fully cooked ham
16 eggs; 2/3 cup sour cream; 1/2 cup 2% milk; 1 teaspoon onion salt; 1/2 teaspoon garlic salt; 1/4 teaspoon pepper
2 cups (8 ounces) shredded cheddar cheese, divided

1. Place potatoes in a small saucepan and cover with water. Bring to a boil. Reduce heat; cover and simmer for 10-15 minutes or until tender. Drain.
2. In a large skillet, saute half of the peppers and onion in 1 teaspoon oil until tender. Add half of the ham and potatoes; saute 2-3 minutes longer.
3. Meanwhile, in a blender, combine eggs, sour cream, milk, onion salt, garlic salt and pepper. Cover and process until smooth.
4. Pour half over vegetable mixture; cook and stir over medium heat until eggs are completely set. Sprinkle with 1 cup cheese. Repeat with remaining ingredients.

Vanilla Fruit Salad

PREP/TOTAL TIME: 20 MIN. MAKES: 10 SERVINGS

Ingredients

1 pound fresh strawberries, quartered
1 1/2 cups seedless red and/or green grapes, halved 2 medium bananas, sliced
2 kiwifruit, peeled, sliced and quartered
1 cup cubed fresh pineapple
1 can (21 ounces) peach pie filling
3 teaspoons vanilla extract

In a large bowl, combine the strawberries, grapes, bananas, kiwi and pineapple. Fold in pie filling and vanilla. Chill until serving.

Colorful Brunch Frittata

PREP: 15 MIN. BAKE: 55 MIN. + STANDING MAKES: 12-15 SERVINGS

Ingredients

1 pound fresh asparagus, trimmed and cut into 1-inch pieces; 1/2 pound sliced fresh mushrooms; 1 medium sweet red pepper, diced; 1 medium sweet yellow pepper, diced; 1 small onion, chopped; 3 green onions, chopped; 3 tablespoons olive oil; 2 garlic cloves, minced; 3 plum tomatoes, seeded and chopped 14 eggs, lightly beaten; 2 cups half-and-half cream 2 cups (8 ounces) shredded Colby-Monterey Jack cheese; 3 tablespoons minced fresh parsley; 3 tablespoons minced fresh basil; 1/2 teaspoon salt; 1/4 teaspoon pepper; 1/2 cup shredded Parmesan cheese

1. In a large skillet, saute the asparagus, mushrooms, peppers and onions in oil until tender. Add garlic; cook 1 minute longer. Add tomatoes; set aside.
2. In a large bowl, whisk the eggs, cream, Colby-Monterey Jack cheese, parsley, basil, salt and pepper; stir into vegetable mixture.
3. Pour into a greased 13-in. x 9-in. baking dish. Bake, uncovered, at 350° for 45 minutes.
4. Sprinkle with Parmesan cheese. Bake 10-15 minutes longer or until a knife inserted near the center comes out clean. Let stand for 10 minutes before cutting.

Hot Fruit Compote

PREP: 15 MIN. BAKE: 40 MIN. MAKES: 20 SERVINGS

Ingredients

2 cans (15 1/4 ounces each) sliced pears, drained
1 can (29 ounces) sliced peaches, drained
1 can (20 ounces) unsweetened pineapple chunks, drained
1 package (20 ounces) pitted dried plums
1 jar (16 ounces) unsweetened applesauce
1 can (21 ounces) cherry pie filling
1/4 cup packed brown sugar

1. In a large bowl, combine the first five ingredients. Pour into a 13-in. x 9-in. baking dish coated with cooking spray. Spread pie filling over fruit mixture; sprinkle with brown sugar.
2. Cover and bake at 350° for 40-45 minutes or until bubbly. Serve warm.

Sage Breakfast Patties

PREP/TOTAL TIME: 30 MIN. MAKES: 1 1/2 DOZEN

Ingredients

2 teaspoons rubbed sage
2 teaspoons minced chives
3/4 teaspoon salt
3/4 teaspoon white pepper
1/4 teaspoon onion powder
1/4 teaspoon chili powder
1/8 teaspoon dried thyme
1 pound ground turkey
1/2 pound ground pork

1. In a large bowl, combine the first seven ingredients. Crumble turkey and pork over mixture and mix well.
2. Shape into eighteen 2-in. patties. In a large skillet, cook patties over medium heat for 3-4 minutes on each side or until thermometer reads 165°. Drain on paper towels.

Gingerbread Pancakes

PREP/TOTAL TIME: 20 MIN. MAKES: 3 SERVINGS

Ingredients

1 cup all-purpose flour
2 tablespoons sugar
1 teaspoon baking powder
1/2 teaspoon ground cinnamon
1/4 teaspoon ground ginger
1/4 teaspoon ground allspice
1 egg
3/4 cup 2% milk
2 tablespoons molasses
1 tablespoon canola oil
6 tablespoons maple pancake syrup
3/4 cup apple pie filling, warmed
3 tablespoons dried cranberries

1. Combine the first six ingredients in large bowl. Combine egg, milk, molasses and oil; stir into dry ingredients just until moistened.
2. Pour batter by 1/4 cupfuls onto a greased hot griddle; turn when bubbles form on top. Cook until the second side is golden brown.
3. To serve, place two pancakes on each plate; drizzle with 2 tablespoons syrup. Top with 1/4 cup apple pie filling; sprinkle with cranberries.

Cinnamon Peach Kuchen

PREP: 25 MIN. BAKE: 45 MIN. + COOLING MAKES: 10 SERVINGS

Ingredients

2 cups all-purpose flour
2 tablespoons sugar
1/2 teaspoon salt
1/4 teaspoon baking powder
1/2 cup cold butter, cubed
2 cans (15 1/4 ounces each) peach halves, drained and patted dry
1 cup packed brown sugar
1 teaspoon ground cinnamon
2 egg yolks, lightly beaten
1 cup heavy whipping cream

1. In a small bowl, combine the flour, sugar, salt and baking powder; cut in butter until crumbly. Press onto the bottom and 1 1/2 in. up the sides of a greased 9-in. springform pan.
2. Place pan on baking sheet. Lay peach halves, cut side up, in crust. Combine brown sugar and cinnamon; sprinkle on top.
3. Bake at 350° for 20 minutes. Combine egg yolks and cream; pour over peaches. Bake 25-30 minutes longer or until top is set. Cool on a wire rack. Refrigerate leftovers.

Christmas Dinner Menus

Peppercorn Beef Top Loin Roast

PREP: 30 MIN. BAKE: 1 HOUR + STANDING MAKES: 10 SERVINGS (1 1/2 CUPS SAUCE)

Ingredients

1 beef top round roast (4 pounds)
1/3 cup packed brown sugar
3 tablespoons whole peppercorns, crushed
4 garlic cloves, minced
3/4 teaspoon salt
1 large onion, finely chopped
1 tablespoon olive oil
2 tablespoons tomato paste
2 teaspoons Worcestershire sauce
1 1/2 cups port wine
1 1/2 cups dry red wine

1. Trim fat from roast. In a small bowl, combine the brown sugar, peppercorns, garlic and salt. Rub over meat. Place in a shallow roasting pan.

2. Bake at 325° for 1 to 1 1/2 hours or until meat reaches desired doneness (for medium-rare, a meat thermometer should read 145°; medium, 160°; well-done, 170°). Let stand for 15 minutes before slicing.

3. Meanwhile, in a large saucepan, saute onion in oil until tender. Stir in tomato paste and Worcestershire sauce until blended. Add wines. Bring to a boil; cook until liquid is reduced to about 1 1/2 cups. Serve with roast.

Garlic Baby Potatoes

PREP: 20 MIN. BAKE: 50 MIN. MAKES: 8 SERVINGS

Ingredients

6 tablespoons olive oil
12 garlic cloves, minced
1/4 cup minced fresh oregano
4 1/2 teaspoons balsamic vinegar
3 teaspoons kosher salt
1 1/2 teaspoons paprika
3/4 teaspoon lemon-pepper seasoning
24 small red or fingerling potatoes, halved

1. In a large bowl, combine the first seven ingredients. Add potatoes; toss to coat. Transfer potatoes to a greased 9-in. square baking pan; drizzle with garlic mixture.
2. Cover and bake at 350° for 40 minutes, stirring every 10 minutes. Uncover; bake 10-20 minutes longer or until potatoes are tender.

Jarlsberg Popovers

PREP: 15 MIN. BAKE: 30 MIN. MAKES: 9 SERVINGS

Ingredients
4 1/2 teaspoons shortening
3 egg whites
2 eggs
1 1/2 cups 2% milk
1/2 cup heavy whipping cream
2 cups all-purpose flour
1 tablespoon sugar
3/4 teaspoon salt
1/4 teaspoon white pepper
4 ounces Jarlsberg cheese, shredded

1. Using 1/2 teaspoon shortening for each cup, grease the bottoms and sides of nine popover cups; set aside.
2. In a small bowl, beat egg whites and eggs; beat in milk and cream. Add the flour, sugar, salt and pepper; beat until smooth (do not overbeat). Fold in cheese. Fill prepared cups two-thirds full with batter. Fill empty cups two-thirds full with water.
3. Bake at 450° for 15 minutes. Reduce heat to 350° (do not open door). Bake 15 minutes longer or until deep golden brown (do not underbake). Immediately cut a slit in the top of each popover to allow steam to escape.

Make Ahead Note: *Make popovers up to a day in advance. Cool completely before storing in an airtight container. Reheat just before serving.*

Zesty Broccolini

PREP/TOTAL TIME: 20 MIN. MAKES: 6 SERVINGS

Ingredients

1 pound Broccolini or broccoli spears
1/2 teaspoon salt
2 garlic cloves, minced
1/2 teaspoon grated fresh gingerroot
3 tablespoons olive oil
1/8 teaspoon crushed red pepper flakes

1. Place Broccolini and salt in a large skillet; cover with water. Bring to a boil. Reduce heat; cover and simmer for 5-7 minutes or until tender. Drain well. Remove and keep warm.
2. In the same skillet, saute the garlic and ginger in oil for 1 minute. Add Broccolini and the pepper flakes; saute for 1-2 minutes or until heated through.

Coconut Cranberry Shortcakes

PREP/TOTAL TIME: 30 MIN. MAKES: 9 SERVINGS

Ingredients

3 cups all-purpose flour; 1/3 cup sugar; 4 teaspoons baking powder; 1 teaspoon salt; 2 cups coconut milk

TOPPING

1 package (12 ounces) fresh or frozen cranberries
1 cup sugar
1/2 cup coconut milk
1/2 cup cranberry juice
Whipped cream, flaked coconut and fresh mint leaves, optional

1. In a large bowl, combine the flour, sugar, baking powder and salt. Stir in coconut milk just until moistened.
2. Drop by 1/3 cupfuls 1 in. apart onto a greased baking sheet. Bake at 400° for 15-20 minutes or until lightly browned.
3. For topping, in a large saucepan, combine the cranberries, sugar, coconut milk and cranberry juice. Cook over medium heat until the berries pop, about 15 minutes.
4. Just before serving, cut shortcakes in half horizontally. Place bottoms on dessert plates; top with half of cranberry mixture. Add tops and remaining cranberry mixture. Garnish with whipped cream, coconut and mint if desired.

Apple Cider-Glazed Ham

PREP: 15 MIN. BAKE: 2 1/2 HOURS MAKES: 10 SERVINGS (1 CUP SAUCE)

Ingredients

1/2 fully cooked bone-in ham (6 to 7 pounds)
2 cups apple cider
1 cup honey
1/2 cup cider vinegar
1/4 cup Dijon mustard
1 tablespoon butter
2 teaspoons chili powder
1/2 teaspoon apple pie spice

1. Place ham on a rack in a shallow roasting pan. Score the surface of the ham, making diamond shapes 1/2 in. deep. Cover and bake at 325° for 2 hours.

2. Meanwhile, in a saucepan, combine the cider, honey, vinegar and mustard; bring to a boil. Reduce heat; simmer, uncovered, for 15 minutes, stirring frequently. Stir in the butter, chili powder and apple pie spice. Set aside 1 cup for serving.

3. Cook the remaining sauce until thickened; spoon over ham. Bake, uncovered, 30-35 minutes longer or until a thermometer reads 140°. Warm reserved sauce; serve with ham.

Merry Berry Salad

PREP/TOTAL TIME: 20 MIN. MAKES: 10 SERVINGS

Ingredients

1 package (10 ounces) mixed salad greens; 1 medium red apple, diced; 1 medium green apple, diced; 1 cup (4 ounces) shredded Parmesan cheese; 1/2 cup dried cranberries; 1/2 cup slivered almonds, toasted

DRESSING

1 cup fresh cranberries

1/2 cup sugar

1/2 cup cider vinegar

1/4 cup thawed apple juice concentrate

1 teaspoon salt

1 teaspoon ground mustard

1 teaspoon grated onion

1 cup canola oil

1. In a large salad bowl, toss the first six ingredients.
2. In a blender, combine the cranberries, sugar, vinegar, apple juice concentrate, salt, mustard and onion; cover and process until blended. While processing, gradually add oil in a steady stream.
3. Drizzle desired amount of dressing over salad and toss to coat. Refrigerate any leftover dressing.

Dijon Green Beans

PREP/TOTAL TIME: 20 MIN. MAKES: 10 SERVINGS

Ingredients

1 1/2 pounds fresh green beans, trimmed
2 tablespoons red wine vinegar
2 tablespoons olive oil
2 teaspoons Dijon mustard
1/2 teaspoon salt
1/4 teaspoon pepper
1 cup grape tomatoes, halved
1/2 small red onion, sliced
2 tablespoons grated Parmesan cheese

1. Place beans in a saucepan and cover with water. Bring to a boil. Cook, covered, for 10-15 minutes or until crisp-tender.
2. Meanwhile, whisk the vinegar, oil, mustard, salt and pepper in a small bowl. Drain beans; place in a large bowl. Add tomatoes and onion. Drizzle with dressing and toss to coat. Sprinkle with cheese.

Bacon Caesar Salad

PREP/TOTAL TIME: 20 MIN. MAKES: 12 SERVINGS (3/4 CUP EACH)

Ingredients

2 cups cubed day-old bread; 2 tablespoons olive oil; 3 garlic cloves, sliced

DRESSING

1/2 cup olive oil; 1/4 cup lemon juice; 1 tablespoon Dijon mustard
3 garlic cloves, minced; 1 1/2 teaspoons anchovy paste
Dash pepper

SALAD

1 large bunch romaine, torn
4 bacon strips, cooked and crumbled
1/2 cup shredded Parmesan cheese

1. In a large skillet, cook bread cubes in oil over medium heat for 4-5 minutes or until golden brown, stirring frequently. Add garlic; cook 1 minute longer. Remove to paper towels; cool.
2. For dressing, in a small bowl, whisk the oil, lemon juice, mustard, garlic, anchovy paste and pepper. In a serving bowl, combine romaine and bacon. Drizzle with dressing; toss to coat. Sprinkle with croutons and cheese.

Make Ahead Note: *Prepare the croutons 1 to 2 days in advance and store in an airtight container.*

Baked Sweet Onions

PREP: 25 MIN. BAKE: 40 MIN. MAKES: 8 SERVINGS

Ingredients

8 large sweet onions, peeled
1/2 cup butter, melted
1/2 cup Burgundy wine or beef broth
8 teaspoons beef bouillon granules
1 teaspoon dried thyme
1 teaspoon pepper
1 1/2 cups shredded Swiss cheese

1. Cut each onion into six wedges to within 1/2 in. of the bottom. Place each onion on a piece of heavy- duty foil (about 12 in. square).
2. In a small bowl, combine the butter, wine, bouillon, thyme and pepper. Spoon over onions; sprinkle with cheese. Fold foil around each onion and seal tightly. Place on a baking sheet. Bake at 425° for 40-45 minutes or until onions are tender. Open foil carefully to allow steam to escape.

Merry Entrees

Cherry-Stuffed Pork Chops

PREP: 20 MIN. GRILL: 20 MIN. MAKES: 6 SERVINGS

Ingredients

1 package (5.6 ounces) couscous with toasted pine nuts
6 boneless pork loin chops (1 inch thick and 6 ounces each)
1/2 cup dried cherries
1 tablespoon brown sugar
1 tablespoon butter, melted
1/2 teaspoon minced fresh gingerroot
1/2 teaspoon garlic powder
1/2 teaspoon pepper

1. Prepare couscous according to package directions. Meanwhile, cut a deep slit in each pork chop, forming a pocket. Stir the cherries, brown sugar, butter and ginger into prepared couscous. Stuff 1/3 cup into each chop; secure with toothpicks. Sprinkle with garlic powder and pepper.
2. Grill pork chops, covered, over medium heat for 10-12 minutes on each side or until a thermometer reads 160°. Discard toothpicks.

Seafood en Croute

PREP: 25 MIN. BAKE: 20 MIN. MAKES: 4 SERVINGS

Ingredients

1 package (17.3 ounces) frozen puff pastry, thawed
4 salmon fillets (6 ounces each)
1/2 pound fresh sea or bay scallops, finely chopped
1/3 cup heavy whipping cream
2 green onions, chopped; 1 tablespoon minced fresh parsley
1/2 teaspoon minced fresh dill; 1/4 teaspoon salt; 1/8 teaspoon pepper; 1 egg white; 1 egg, lightly beaten

1. On a lightly floured surface, roll each pastry sheet into a 12-in. x 10-in. rectangle. Cut each sheet into four 6-in. x 5-in. rectangles. Place a salmon fillet in the center of four rectangles.

2. In a large bowl, combine the scallops, cream, onions, parsley, dill, salt and pepper. In a small bowl, beat egg white on medium speed until soft peaks form; fold into scallop mixture. Spoon about 1/2 cup over each salmon fillet.

3. Top each with a pastry rectangle and crimp to seal. With a small sharp knife, cut several slits in the top. Place in a greased 15-in. x 10-in. x 1-in. baking pan; brush with egg.

4. Bake at 400° for 20-25 minutes or until a thermometer reads 160°.

Baked Lobster Tails

PREP: 15 MIN. BAKE: 20 MIN. MAKES: 6 SERVINGS

Ingredients

3 lobster tails (8 to 10 ounces each)
1 cup water
1 tablespoon minced fresh parsley
1/8 teaspoon salt
Dash pepper
1 tablespoon butter, melted
2 tablespoons lemon juice
Lemon wedges and additional melted butter, optional

1. Split lobster tails in half lengthwise. With cut side up and using scissors, cut along the edge of shell to loosen the cartilage covering the tail meat from the shell; remove and discard cartilage.
2. Pour water into a 13-in. x 9-in. baking dish; place lobster tails in dish. Combine the parsley, salt and pepper; sprinkle over lobster. Drizzle with butter and lemon juice.
3. Bake, uncovered, at 375° for 20-25 minutes or until meat is firm and opaque. Serve with lemon and melted butter if desired.

Spinach Steak Pinwheels

PREP/TOTAL TIME: 30 MIN. MAKES: 4 SERVINGS

Ingredients

1 beef flank steak (1 1/2 pounds)
1 package (10 ounces) frozen chopped spinach, thawed and squeezed dry
1/4 cup grated Parmesan cheese
1/4 cup sour cream
Dash each salt and pepper

1. Cut steak horizontally from a long side to within 1/2 in. of opposite side. Open meat so it lies flat; cover with plastic wrap. Flatten to 1/4-in. thickness. Remove plastic.
2. In a small bowl, combine the spinach, cheese and sour cream; spread over steak to within 1/2 in. of edges. With the grain of the meat going from left to right, roll up jelly-roll style. Slice beef across the grain into eight slices.
3. Transfer to an ungreased baking sheet. Sprinkle with salt and pepper. Broil 4-6 in. from the heat for 5-7 minutes on each side or until meat reaches desired doneness (for medium-rare, a thermometer should read 145°; medium, 160°; well-done, 170°).

Spiral Ham with Cranberry Glaze

PREP: 15 MIN. BAKE: 3 HOURS MAKES: 12-16 SERVINGS

Ingredients

1 bone-in fully cooked spiral-sliced ham (8 pounds)
1 can (14 ounces) whole-berry cranberry sauce
1 package (12 ounces) fresh or frozen cranberries
1 jar (12 ounces) red currant jelly
1 cup light corn syrup
1/2 teaspoon ground ginger

1. Place ham on a rack in a shallow roasting pan. Cover and bake at 325° for 21/2 hours.
2. Meanwhile, for glaze, combine the remaining ingredients in a saucepan. Bring to a boil. Reduce heat; simmer, uncovered, until cranberries pop, stirring occasionally. Remove from the heat; set aside.
3. Uncover ham; bake 30 minutes longer or until a thermometer reads 140°, basting twice with 11/2 cups glaze. Serve remaining glaze with ham.

Garlic Pork Roast

PREP: 10 MIN. BAKE: 1 HOUR 30 MIN. + STANDING MAKES: 8 SERVINGS

Ingredients

1 bone-in pork loin roast (5 pounds)
1/2 medium green pepper, finely chopped
1/2 cup thinly sliced green onions
1/2 cup chopped celery
8 garlic cloves, minced
1 teaspoon salt
1/4 teaspoon cayenne pepper

1. With a sharp knife, cut a deep pocket between each rib on meaty side of roast. In a small bowl, mix the green pepper, green onions, celery and garlic; stuff into pockets. Sprinkle salt and cayenne pepper over roast.
2. Place roast in a shallow roasting pan, stuffing side up. Roast at 350° for 1 1/2 to 1 3/4 hours or until a thermometer inserted in pork reads 145°. Remove roast from oven; tent with foil. Let stand for 15 minutes before carving.

Duck with Cherry Sauce

PREP: 15 MIN. BAKE: 2 HOURS + STANDING MAKES: 4-5 SERVINGS

Ingredients

1 domestic duckling (4 to 5 pounds)
1 jar (12 ounces) cherry preserves
1 to 2 tablespoons red wine vinegar

1. Prick skin of duckling well and place breast side up on a rack in a shallow roasting pan. Tie drumsticks together. Bake, uncovered, at 350° for 2 to 2 1/2 hours or until juices run clear and a thermometer reads 180°. (Drain fat from pan as it accumulates.) Cover and let stand 20 minutes before carving.

2. Meanwhile, for sauce, combine preserves and vinegar in a small saucepan. Cook and stir over medium heat until heated through. Serve with duck.

Baked Ham with Orange Glaze

PREP: 5 MIN. BAKE: 1 HOUR 50 MIN. + STANDING MAKES: 10 SERVINGS

Ingredients

1 fully cooked bone-in ham (6 to 7 pounds)
2 cups apple cider or unsweetened juice
2 cups orange juice
1/3 cup orange marmalade
1/4 cup packed brown sugar
1/4 cup Dijon mustard
1/4 teaspoon ground ginger

1. Place ham on a rack in a shallow roasting pan. Score the surface of the ham, making diamond shapes 1/4 in. deep. Add cider and orange juice to pan. Loosely cover ham with foil; bake at 325° for 1 hour. Combine remaining ingredients; brush some over ham.
2. Bake, uncovered, 50-60 minutes longer or until a thermometer reads 140°, brushing occasionally with glaze. Serve with remaining glaze.

Pesto Pepper Tortellini

PREP/TOTAL TIME: 20 MIN. MAKES: 4 SERVINGS

Ingredients

1 package (19 ounces) frozen cheese tortellini
1/2 cup julienned sweet red pepper
1/2 cup butter
3 garlic cloves, minced
2 cups heavy whipping cream
1/4 cup ground walnuts
2 tablespoons minced fresh basil or 2 teaspoons dried basil
1 tablespoon chopped green onion or chives

1. Prepare tortellini according to package directions.
2. Meanwhile, in a large skillet, saute red pepper in butter until pepper is crisp-tender. Add garlic; cook 1 minute longer. Stir in the cream; cook for 8-10 minutes or until slightly thickened.
3. Add the walnuts, basil and onion; heat through. Drain tortellini; add to sauce and toss to coat.

Champagne Baked Ham

PREP: 10 MIN. BAKE: 2 HOURS MAKES: 18 SERVINGS

Ingredients

1 boneless fully cooked ham (9 pounds)
1 1/2 cups champagne
3/4 cup packed brown sugar
4 1/2 teaspoons honey
3/4 teaspoon ground ginger 3/4 teaspoon ground mustard

1. Place ham on a rack in a shallow roasting pan. Score the surface of the ham, making diamond shapes 1/2 in. deep. Bake, uncovered, at 325° for 1 1/2 hours.
2. Meanwhile, in a small saucepan, combine the remaining ingredients. Bring to a boil; cook until glaze is reduced by half. Remove from the heat.
3. Baste ham with glaze; bake 30 minutes longer or until a thermometer reads 140°, basting twice with glaze. Serve with the remaining glaze.

Jolly Sides

Company's Coming Salad

PREP/TOTAL TIME: 30 MIN. MAKES: 8 SERVINGS

Ingredients

2 tablespoons sugar
1/2 cup sliced almonds
1 package (5 ounces) spring mix salad greens
6 cups torn romaine
1 can (11 ounces) mandarin oranges, drained
2 celery ribs, thinly sliced
1 small red onion, chopped
2 green onions, thinly sliced

DRESSING

3 tablespoons canola oil
2 tablespoons cider vinegar
5 teaspoons sugar
1 tablespoon minced fresh parsley
1/4 teaspoon salt

1. In a small heavy skillet, cook and stir the sugar over medium-low heat until melted. Stir in almonds; cook for 1 minute or until lightly browned. Spread onto foil coated with cooking spray; set aside.
2. In a large salad bowl, combine the mixed greens, romaine, oranges, celery and onions. In a small bowl, whisk the dressing ingredients. Drizzle over salad; add almonds and toss to coat.

Beans with Parsley Sauce

PREP/TOTAL TIME: 30 MIN. MAKES: 8 SERVINGS

Ingredients

2 pounds fresh green beans, trimmed
2 tablespoons butter
2 tablespoons all-purpose flour
1 teaspoon salt
1/8 teaspoon pepper
1 1/2 cups chicken broth
2 egg yolks
1/2 cup 2% milk
1 cup minced fresh parsley

1. Place beans in a large saucepan and cover with water; bring to a boil. Cook, uncovered, for 8-10 minutes or until crisp-tender. Meanwhile, in a large skillet, melt butter over medium heat. Stir in the flour, salt and pepper until smooth. Gradually whisk in broth. Bring to a boil; cook and stir for 1-2 minutes or until thickened. Remove from the heat.

2. In a small bowl, combine egg yolks and milk. Stir a small amount of hot broth mixture into egg mixture. Return all to the pan, stirring constantly. Bring to a gentle boil; cook and stir for 2 minutes or until thickened and coats the back of a metal spoon. Stir in parsley. Drain beans; serve with sauce.

Gingered Orange Beets

PREP: 10 MIN. BAKE: 70 MIN. MAKES: 4 SERVINGS

Ingredients

1 1/2 pounds whole fresh beets (about 4 medium), trimmed and cleaned
6 tablespoons olive oil, divided
1/4 teaspoon salt
1/4 teaspoon white pepper
1 tablespoon rice vinegar
1 tablespoon thawed orange juice concentrate
1 1/2 teaspoons grated orange peel, divided
1/2 teaspoon minced fresh gingerroot
1 medium navel orange, peeled, sectioned and chopped
1/3 cup pecan halves, toasted

1. Brush beets with 4 tablespoons oil; sprinkle with salt and pepper. Wrap loosely in foil; place on a baking sheet. Bake at 425° for 70-75 minutes or until fork-tender. Cool slightly.
2. In a small bowl, whisk the vinegar, orange juice concentrate, 1 teaspoon orange peel, ginger and remaining oil; set aside.
3. Peel beets and cut into wedges; place in a serving bowl. Add the orange sections and pecans. Drizzle with orange sauce and toss to coat. Sprinkle with remaining orange peel.

Spinach Almond Salad

PREP/TOTAL TIME: 15 MIN. MAKES: 8 SERVINGS

Ingredients

1 package (6 ounces) fresh baby spinach
2 large tart apples, thinly sliced
10 bacon strips, cooked and crumbled
1 cup dried cranberries
3/4 cup slivered almonds, toasted
VINAIGRETTE
1/4 cup sugar
3 tablespoons cider vinegar
2 teaspoons finely chopped onion
1/4 teaspoon salt
1/3 cup olive oil

In a large bowl, combine the first five ingredients. In a blender, combine the sugar, vinegar, onion and salt; cover and process until blended. While processing, gradually add oil in a steady stream. Pour over salad; toss to coat.

Black-Eyed Peas with Bacon

PREP: 10 MIN. + SOAKING COOK: 35 MIN. MAKES: 8 SERVINGS

Ingredients

1 pound dried black-eyed peas, rinsed and sorted
1/2 pound bacon, cooked and crumbled
1 tablespoon butter
1 large onion, chopped
1 garlic clove, minced
1/2 teaspoon dried thyme
Salt to taste
Additional cooked and crumbled bacon, optional

1. Place peas and bacon in a large Dutch oven; add water to cover. Bring to a boil; boil for 2 minutes. Remove from the heat; let soak, covered, for 1 hour. Do not drain.
2. In a skillet, heat butter over medium-high heat. Add onion; cook and stir until tender. Add garlic; cook 1 minute longer. Stir in thyme and salt.
3. Add to pea mixture; return to the heat. Cook, covered, over medium heat for 30 minutes or until peas are tender, stirring occasionally. If desired, top with additional crumbled bacon.

Cranberry Gelatin Mold

PREP: 15 MIN. + CHILLING, MAKES: 8 SERVINGS

Ingredients

2 packages (3 ounces each) raspberry gelatin
3 cups boiling water
1 can (14 ounces) whole-berry cranberry sauce
2 tablespoons lemon juice
1 can (8 ounces) unsweetened crushed pineapple, drained
1/2 cup finely chopped celery

1. In a large bowl, dissolve gelatin in boiling water. Stir in cranberry sauce and lemon juice until blended. Chill until partially set.
2. Stir in pineapple and celery. Pour into a 6-cup ring mold coated with cooking spray. Refrigerate until firm. Unmold onto a serving platter.

Marinated Italian Salad

PREP: 30 MIN. + MARINATING MAKES: 12 SERVINGS

Ingredients

4 cups fresh broccoli florets
3 cups fresh cauliflowerets
1/2 pound sliced fresh mushrooms
2 celery ribs, chopped
4 green onions, thinly sliced
1 can (8 ounces) sliced water chestnuts, drained
1 bottle (16 ounces) Italian salad dressing
1 envelope Italian salad dressing mix
1 pint cherry tomatoes, halved
1 can (2 1/4 ounces) sliced ripe olives, drained

1. In a large serving bowl, combine the broccoli, cauliflower, mushrooms, celery, onions and water chestnuts. In a small bowl, whisk salad dressing and dressing mix; drizzle over vegetables and toss to coat.
2. Cover and refrigerate overnight. Just before serving, add tomatoes and olives; toss to coat.

Peas in Cheese Sauce

PREP/TOTAL TIME: 20 MIN. MAKES: 8 SERVINGS

Ingredients

4 1/2 teaspoons butter
4 1/2 teaspoons all-purpose flour
1/4 teaspoon salt
1/8 teaspoon white pepper
1 1/2 cups 2% milk
3/4 cup cubed process cheese (Velveeta)
2 packages (10 ounces each) frozen peas, thawed

In a large saucepan, melt butter over low heat. Stir in the flour, salt and pepper until smooth. Gradually add milk. Bring to a boil; cook and stir for 2 minutes or until thickened. Add the cheese; stir until melted. Stir in peas; cook 1-2 minutes longer or until heated through.

Baked Rice Pilaf

PREP: 10 MIN. BAKE: 40 MIN. MAKES: 4 SERVINGS

Ingredients

1 3/4 cups water
1 cup shredded carrot
1 cup chopped celery
3/4 cup uncooked long grain rice
3 tablespoons minced fresh parsley
2 tablespoons finely chopped onion
2 tablespoons butter, melted
1 tablespoon chicken bouillon granules

In an ungreased 8-in. square baking dish, combine all the ingredients. Cover and bake at 375° for 40- 45 minutes or until rice is tender, stirring after 25 minutes.

Balsamic-Glazed Brussels Sprouts

PREP/TOTAL TIME: 30 MIN. MAKES: 8 SERVINGS

Ingredients

2 pounds fresh Brussels sprouts
1/2 pound bacon strips, cut into 1/2-inch pieces
1 medium onion, sliced
1/4 cup white balsamic vinegar
2 tablespoons stone-ground mustard
1/2 teaspoon garlic powder
1/8 teaspoon salt
1/2 cup soft bread crumbs

1. Cut an "X" in the core of each Brussels sprout. Place in a large saucepan; add 1 in. of water. Bring to a boil. Reduce heat; cover and simmer for 8-10 minutes or until crisp-tender.
2. Meanwhile, in a large ovenproof skillet, cook bacon over medium heat until crisp. Using a slotted spoon, remove to paper towels; drain, reserving 2 tablespoons drippings.
3. Saute onion in drippings until tender. Stir in the vinegar, mustard, garlic powder, salt, Brussels sprouts and bacon; cook 2-3 minutes longer.
4. Sprinkle with bread crumbs; broil 4-6 in. from the heat for 2-3 minutes or until golden brown.

Glorious Breads

Merry Christmas Scones

PREP: 25 MIN. BAKE: 15 MIN. MAKES: 1 DOZEN

Ingredients

2 cups all-purpose flour
3 teaspoons baking powder
1/2 teaspoon salt
2 tablespoons cold butter
1 cup eggnog
1 cup chopped pecans
1/2 cup red candied cherries, quartered
1/2 cup green candied cherries, quartered

GLAZE

1/2 cup confectioners' sugar
1 teaspoon rum extract
4 to 5 teaspoons heavy whipping cream

1. In a large bowl, combine the flour, baking powder and salt; cut in butter until mixture resembles coarse crumbs. Stir in eggnog just until moistened. Stir in pecans and candied cherries.

2. Turn onto a floured surface; knead 10 times. Transfer dough to a greased baking sheet. Pat into a 9- in. circle. Cut into 12 wedges, but do not separate.

3. Bake at 425° for 12-14 minutes or until golden brown. Combine glaze ingredients; drizzle over scones. Serve warm.

Multigrain Bread

PREP: 10 MIN. BAKE: 3-4 HOURS MAKES: 1 LOAF (2 POUNDS)

Ingredients

1 cup water (70° to 80°)
2 tablespoons canola oil
2 egg yolks
1/4 cup molasses
1 teaspoon salt
1 1/2 cups bread flour
1 cup whole wheat flour
1/2 cup rye flour
1/2 cup nonfat dry milk powder
1/4 cup quick-cooking oats
1/4 cup toasted wheat germ
1/4 cup cornmeal
2 1/4 teaspoons active dry yeast

1. In bread machine pan, place all ingredients in order suggested by manufacturer. Select basic bread setting. Choose crust color and loaf size if available.

2. Bake according to bread machine directions (check dough after 5 minutes of mixing; add 1 to 2 tablespoons water or flour if needed).

Editor's Note: *We recommend you do not use a bread machine's time-delay feature for this recipe.*

Cracked Pepper Cheddar Muffins

PREP: 15 MIN. BAKE: 25 MIN. MAKES: 1 DOZEN

Ingredients

2 cups all-purpose flour
1 tablespoon sugar
3 teaspoons baking powder
1/2 teaspoon coarsely ground pepper
1 egg
1 1/4 cups 2% milk
2 tablespoons canola oil
1 cup (4 ounces) shredded cheddar cheese

1. In a large bowl, combine the flour, sugar, baking powder and pepper. In another bowl, whisk the egg, milk and oil. Stir into dry ingredients just until moistened. Fold in cheese.

2. Fill muffins cups coated with cooking spray two-thirds full. Bake at 375° for 25-30 minutes or until a toothpick inserted near the center comes out clean. Cool for 5 minutes before removing from pan to a wire rack. Serve warm.

Grandma's Honey Muffins

PREP/TOTAL TIME: 30 MIN. MAKES: 1 DOZEN

Ingredients

2 cups all-purpose flour
1/2 cup sugar
3 teaspoons baking powder
1/2 teaspoon salt
1 egg
1 cup 2% milk
1/4 cup butter, melted
1/4 cup honey

1. In a large bowl, combine the flour, sugar, baking powder and salt. In a small bowl, combine the egg, milk, butter and honey. Stir into dry ingredients just until moistened.
2. Fill greased or paper-lined muffin cups three-fourths full. Bake at 400° for 15-18 minutes or until a toothpick inserted near the center comes out clean. Remove from pan to a wire rack. Serve warm.

Mini Toffee Rolls

PREP: 20 MIN. BAKE: 15 MIN. MAKES: 4 DOZEN

Ingredients

6 tablespoons butter, softened
1/2 cup packed brown sugar
1 teaspoon ground cinnamon
1/3 cup milk chocolate English toffee bits
2 tubes (8 ounces each) refrigerated crescent rolls
1 cup confectioners' sugar
4 1/2 teaspoons 2% milk
1/4 teaspoon vanilla extract

1. In a small bowl, cream the butter, brown sugar and cinnamon until light and fluffy. Stir in toffee bits.
2. Separate each tube of crescent dough into four rectangles; seal perforations. Spread evenly with butter mixture. Roll up each rectangle jelly-roll style, starting with a long side.
3. Cut each into six 1-in. slices; place cut side down into two greased 8-in. square baking dishes. Bake at 375° for 14-16 minutes or until golden brown.
4. In a small bowl, combine the confectioners' sugar, milk and vanilla until smooth. Drizzle over warm rolls.

Apple Spice Muffins

PREP: 15 MIN. BAKE: 20 MIN. MAKES: 1 DOZEN

Ingredients

2 cups all-purpose flour
1 cup granola without raisins
2/3 cup sugar
3 teaspoons baking powder
1 teaspoon salt
1/2 teaspoon ground cinnamon
1/4 teaspoon ground nutmeg
2 eggs
2/3 cup unsweetened apple juice
1/4 cup canola oil
1 1/2 cups grated peeled apples

1. In a large bowl, combine the first seven ingredients. In another bowl, whisk the eggs, apple juice and oil. Stir into dry ingredients just until moistened. Fold in apples.

2. Fill greased or paper-lined muffin cups three-fourths full. Bake at 400° for 18-20 minutes or until a toothpick inserted near the center comes out clean. Cool for 5 minutes before removing from pan to a wire rack. Serve warm.

Cheddar Garlic Biscuits

PREP/TOTAL TIME: 25 MIN. MAKES: 15 BISCUITS

Ingredients

2 cups biscuit/baking mix
1/2 cup shredded cheddar cheese
1/2 teaspoon dried minced onion
2/3 cup 2% milk
1/4 cup butter, melted
1/2 teaspoon garlic powder

1. Combine the biscuit mix, cheese and onion in a large bowl. Stir in milk until a soft dough forms; stir 30 seconds longer.
2. Drop by rounded tablespoonfuls 2 in. apart onto ungreased baking sheets. Bake at 450° for 8-10 minutes or until golden brown. Combine butter and garlic powder; brush over biscuits. Serve warm.

Sweet Potato Biscuits

PREP/TOTAL TIME: 30 MIN. MAKES: 1 1/2 DOZEN

Ingredients

2 cups self-rising flour
1/8 teaspoon salt
1/2 cup shortening
1 cup mashed sweet potatoes
4 to 5 tablespoons 2% milk

1. In a large bowl, combine flour and salt. Cut in shortening and sweet potatoes until mixture resembles coarse crumbs. Stir in enough milk just until dough clings together. Knead lightly on a floured surface.
2. Roll dough to 1/2-in. thickness. Cut with a 2-in. biscuit cutter and place on a lightly greased baking sheet. Bake at 450° for 12 minutes or until golden brown. Serve warm.

Editor's Note: *As a substitute for each cup of self-rising flour, place 1 1/2 teaspoons baking powder and 1/2 teaspoon salt in a measuring cup. Add all-purpose flour to measure 1 cup.*

Lemony Poppy Seed Muffins

PREP: 25 MIN. BAKE: 20 MIN. MAKES: 6 JUMBO MUFFINS

Ingredients

1/2 cup butter, softened
3/4 cup sugar
2 eggs
3/4 cup sour cream
1/4 cup lemon juice
3 teaspoons lemon extract
1 teaspoon vanilla extract
1 teaspoon grated lemon peel
2 cups all-purpose flour
1 teaspoon baking powder
1 teaspoon baking soda
1/4 teaspoon salt
2 tablespoons poppy seeds

1. In a large bowl, cream butter and sugar until light and fluffy. Add eggs, one at a time, beating well after each addition. Beat in the sour cream, lemon juice, extracts and lemon peel.
2. Combine the flour, baking powder, baking soda and salt; gradually add to creamed mixture just until moistened. Fold in poppy seeds.
3. Fill six greased jumbo muffin pans. Bake at 375° for 20-23 minutes or until a toothpick inserted near the center comes out clean. Remove to a wire rack. Serve warm.

Sweet Potato Rolls

PREP: 15 MIN. + RISING BAKE: 10 MIN./BATCH MAKES: 2 1/2 DOZEN

Ingredients

1/2 cup water (70° to 80°)
1 egg
3 tablespoons butter, softened
3/4 cup mashed sweet potatoes (without added milk and butter)
4 to 4 1/2 cups all-purpose flour
3 tablespoons sugar
1 1/2 teaspoons salt
2 packages (1/4 ounce each) active dry yeast

1. In bread machine pan, place all ingredients in order suggested by manufacturer. Select dough setting (check dough after 5 minutes of mixing; add 1 to 2 tablespoons of water or flour if needed).

2. When cycle is completed, turn dough onto a lightly floured surface. Punch down. Divide into 30 portions; roll each into a ball. Place on greased baking sheets. Cover and let rise in a warm place until doubled, about 30 minutes.

3. Bake at 400° for 8-10 minutes or until golden brown. Serve warm.

Editor's Note: *We recommend you do not use a bread machine's time-delay feature for this recipe.*

Yuletide Cookies & Bars

Orange-Cinnamon Chocolate Chip Cookies

PREP: 15 MIN. + CHILLING BAKE: 15 MIN./BATCH MAKES: ABOUT 3 DOZEN

Ingredients

1 cup butter, softened
3/4 cup sugar
3/4 cup packed brown sugar
2 eggs
1 tablespoon grated orange peel
1 teaspoon vanilla extract
3 1/2 cups all-purpose flour
1 1/2 teaspoons baking soda
1 1/4 teaspoons ground cinnamon
3/4 teaspoon salt
2 cups (12 ounces) semisweet chocolate chips
1 cup chopped walnuts

1. In a large bowl, cream butter and sugars until light and fluffy. Beat in the eggs, orange peel and vanilla. Combine the flour, baking soda, cinnamon and salt; gradually add to the creamed mixture and mix well. Stir in the chips and walnuts. Cover and chill for 2 hours or until easy to handle.

2. On lightly floured surface, roll out dough to 1/2-in. thickness. Cut with a lightly floured 3-in. round cookie cutter. Place 1 in. apart on greased baking sheets.

3. Bake at 375° for 12-14 minutes or until lightly browned. Remove to wire racks to cool.

Coconut Crunch Cookies

PREP: 30 MIN. BAKE: 10 MIN./BATCH MAKES: ABOUT 4 1/2 DOZEN

Ingredients

1 cup butter, softened
3/4 cup sugar
3/4 cup packed brown sugar
2 eggs
2 teaspoons vanilla extract
1 teaspoon almond extract
2 cups all-purpose flour
1 teaspoon baking soda
3/4 teaspoon salt
2 cups flaked coconut
1 package (11 1/2 ounces) milk chocolate chips
1 1/2 cups finely chopped almonds

1. In a large bowl, cream butter and sugars until light and fluffy. Beat in eggs and extracts. Combine the flour, baking soda and salt; gradually add to creamed mixture and mix well. Stir in the coconut, chocolate chips and almonds.

2. Drop by rounded teaspoonfuls 2 in. apart onto ungreased baking sheets. Bake at 375° for 9-11 minutes or until lightly browned. Cool for 1 minute before removing from pans to wire racks.

Snickerdoodles

PREP/TOTAL TIME: 25 MIN. MAKES: 2 1/2 DOZEN

Ingredients

1/2 cup butter, softened
1 cup plus 2 tablespoons sugar, divided
1 egg
1/2 teaspoon vanilla extract
1 1/2 cups all-purpose flour
1/4 teaspoon baking soda
1/4 teaspoon cream of tartar
1 teaspoon ground cinnamon

1. In a large bowl, cream butter and 1 cup sugar until light and fluffy. Beat in egg and vanilla. Combine the flour, baking soda and cream of tartar; gradually add to the creamed mixture and mix well. In a small bowl, combine cinnamon and remaining sugar.
2. Shape dough into 1-in. balls; roll in cinnamon-sugar. Place 2 in. apart on ungreased baking sheets. Bake at 375° for 10-12 minutes or until lightly browned. Remove to wire racks to cool.

Decorated Christmas Cutout Cookies

PREP: 15 MIN. + CHILLINGBAKE: 10 MIN./BATCH + COOLINGMAKES: 6-7 DOZEN (21/2-IN. COOKIES)

Ingredients

3/4 cup butter, softened
1 cup sugar
2 eggs
1 teaspoon vanilla extract
2 3/4 cups all-purpose flour 1 teaspoon baking powder
1/2 teaspoon salt
Tinted frostings, colored sugars, edible glitter and nonpareils

1. In a large bowl, cream butter and sugar until light and fluffy. Beat in eggs and vanilla. Combine the flour, baking powder and salt; gradually add to creamed mixture and mix well. Refrigerate for 1 hour or until firm.
2. On a lightly floured surface, roll out dough to 1/4-in. thickness. Cut out with Christmas cookie cutters of your choice. Using a floured spatula, transfer cookies to greased baking sheets.
3. Bake at 375° for 8-10 minutes or until lightly browned. Cool completely on wire racks.
4. Decorate cookies with frosting, sugars and candies.

Slice 'n' Bake Fruitcake Cookies

PREP: 20 MIN. + CHILLING BAKE: 15 MIN./BATCH MAKES: 5 DOZEN

Ingredients

1 cup butter, softened
1 cup confectioners' sugar
1/2 cup sugar
1 egg
2 teaspoons vanilla extract
2 1/4 cups all-purpose flour
1/2 teaspoon baking soda
1/2 cup raisins
1/2 cup each red and green candied cherries, chopped

1. In a large bowl, cream butter and sugars until light and fluffy. Beat in egg and vanilla. Combine flour and baking soda; gradually add to creamed mixture and mix well. Fold in raisins and cherries.

2. Shape dough into two 2-in.-thick logs; wrap each in plastic wrap. Refrigerate for 2 hours or until firm.

3. Cut logs into 1/4-in. slices. Place 2 in. apart on ungreased baking sheets. Bake at 350° for 12-15 minutes or until lightly browned. Remove to wire racks to cool.

Polka-Dot Macaroons

PREP: 15 MIN. BAKE: 10 MIN./BATCH MAKES: ABOUT 4 1/2 DOZEN

Ingredients

5 cups flaked coconut
1 can (14 ounces) sweetened condensed milk
1/2 cup all-purpose flour
1 1/2 cups M & M's minis

1. In a large bowl, combine the coconut, milk and flour. Stir in M&M's.
2. Drop by rounded tablespoonfuls 2 in. apart onto baking sheets coated with cooking spray. Bake at 350° for 8-10 minutes or until edges are lightly browned. Remove to wire racks.

Cherry Kisses

PREP: 10 MIN. BAKE: 20 MIN./BATCH MAKES: 6 DOZEN

Ingredients

4 egg whites
1 1/4 cups sugar
1/3 cup chopped walnuts
1/3 cup chopped pitted dates
1/3 cup chopped candied cherries

1. Place egg whites in a large bowl; let stand at room temperature for 30 minutes. Beat on medium speed until soft peaks form. Gradually beat in sugar, 1 tablespoon at a time, on high until stiff glossy peaks form and the sugar is dissolved. Fold in the walnuts, dates and cherries.
2. Drop by teaspoonfuls 2 in. apart onto lightly greased baking sheets. Bake at 300° for 20-30 minutes or until firm to the touch. Cool for 1 minute before removing to a wire rack. Store in an airtight container.

Peppermint Meltaways

PREP: 30 MIN. BAKE: 10 MIN./BATCH + COOLING MAKES: 3 1/2 DOZEN

Ingredients

1 cup butter, softened
1/2 cup confectioners' sugar
1/2 teaspoon peppermint extract 1
1/4 cups all-purpose flour
1/2 cup cornstarch

FROSTING

2 tablespoons butter, softened
1 1/2 cups confectioners' sugar
2 tablespoons 2% milk
1/4 teaspoon peppermint extract
2 to 3 drops red food coloring, optional
1/2 cup crushed peppermint candies

1. In a small bowl, cream butter and confectioners' sugar until light and fluffy. Beat in extract. Combine flour and cornstarch; gradually add to creamed mixture and mix well.

2. Shape into 1-in. balls. Place 2 in. apart on ungreased baking sheets. Bake at 350° for 10-12 minutes or until bottoms are lightly browned. Remove to wire racks to cool.

3. In a small bowl, beat butter until fluffy. Add the confectioners' sugar, milk, extract and, if desired, food coloring; beat until smooth. Spread over cooled cookies; sprinkle with crushed candies. Store in an airtight container.

Date Nut Icebox Cookies

PREP: 15 MIN. + CHILLING BAKE: 10 MIN./BATCH MAKES: ABOUT 8 DOZEN

Ingredients

1 cup butter, softened
1 cup shortening
2 1/2 cups sugar
2 eggs
1 1/2 teaspoons vanilla extract
1 tablespoon light corn syrup
5 cups all-purpose flour
1 teaspoon salt
1 teaspoon baking soda
1 cup finely chopped walnuts 1 cup finely chopped dates

1. In a large bowl, cream the butter, shortening and sugar until light and fluffy. Add eggs, one at a time, beating well after each addition. Beat in vanilla and corn syrup. Combine the flour, salt and baking soda; gradually add to the creamed mixture and mix well. Stir in walnuts and dates.
2. Shape into four 6-in. rolls; wrap each in plastic wrap. Refrigerate overnight.
3. Unwrap and cut into 1/4-in. slices. Place 2 1/2 in. apart on ungreased baking sheets. Bake at 375° for 10-12 minutes or until lightly browned. Cool for 2-3 minutes before removing to wire racks.

Gingerbread Cookies

PREP: 30 MIN. + CHILLING BAKE: 10 MIN./BATCH + COOLING MAKES: 5 DOZEN

Ingredients

3/4 cup butter, softened
1 cup packed brown sugar
1 egg
3/4 cup molasses
4 cups all-purpose flour
2 teaspoons ground ginger
1 1/2 teaspoons baking soda
1 1/2 teaspoons ground cinnamon
3/4 teaspoon ground cloves
1/4 teaspoon salt
Vanilla frosting of your choice
Red and green paste food coloring

1. In a large bowl, cream butter and brown sugar until light and fluffy. Add egg and molasses. Combine the flour, ginger, baking soda, cinnamon, cloves and salt; gradually add to creamed mixture and mix well. Cover and refrigerate for 4 hours or overnight or until easy to handle.

2. On a lightly floured surface, roll dough to 1/8-in. thickness. Cut with floured 2 1/2-in. cookie cutters. Place 1 in. apart on ungreased baking sheets.

3. Bake at 350° for 8-10 minutes or until edges are firm. Remove to wire racks to cool. Tint some of the frosting red and some green. Decorate cookies.

Heavenly Desserts

Pumpkin Pound Cake

PREP: 10 MIN. BAKE: 1 HOUR + COOLING MAKES: 12-16 SERVINGS

Ingredients

2 1/2 cups sugar
1 cup canola oil
3 eggs
3 cups all-purpose flour
2 teaspoons baking soda
1 teaspoon ground cinnamon
1 teaspoon ground nutmeg
1/2 teaspoon salt
1/4 teaspoon ground cloves
1 can (15 ounces) solid-pack pumpkin
Confectioners' sugar

1. In a large bowl, combine sugar and oil until blended. Add eggs, one at a time, beating well after each addition. Combine the flour, baking soda, cinnamon, nutmeg, salt and cloves; add to egg mixture alternately with pumpkin, beating well after each addition.
2. Transfer to a greased 10-in. fluted tube pan. Bake at 350° for 60-65 minutes or until toothpick inserted near the center comes out clean. Cool for 10 minutes before inverting onto a wire rack. Remove pan and cool completely. Dust with confectioners' sugar.

Peppermint Puff Pastry Sticks

PREP: 15 MIN. BAKE: 15 MIN./BATCH + COOLING MAKES: ABOUT 3 DOZEN

Ingredients

1 sheet frozen puff pastry, thawed
10 ounces milk chocolate candy coating, coarsely chopped
1 1/2 cups crushed peppermint candies

1. Unfold pastry sheet onto a lightly floured surface. Cut into 4-in. x 1/2-in. strips. Place on greased baking sheets. Bake strips at 400° for 12-15 minutes or until golden brown. Remove to wire racks to cool.

2. In a microwave, melt candy coating; stir until smooth. Dip each cookie halfway, allowing excess to drip off. Sprinkle with crushed candies. Place on waxed paper; let stand until set. Store in an airtight container.

Apple Pie in a Goblet

PREP: 10 MIN. COOK: 25 MIN. MAKES: 4 SERVINGS

Ingredients

3 large tart apples, peeled and chopped
1/4 cup sugar
1/4 cup water
3/4 teaspoon ground cinnamon
1/4 teaspoon ground nutmeg
12 shortbread cookies, crushed
2 cups vanilla ice cream
Whipped cream

1. In a large saucepan, combine the apples, sugar, water, cinnamon and nutmeg. Bring to a boil. Reduce heat; cover and simmer for 10 minutes or until apples are tender. Uncover; cook 9-11 minutes longer or until most of the liquid has evaporated. Remove from the heat.

2. In each of four goblets or parfait glasses, layer 1 tablespoon cookie crumbs, the ice cream and the apple mixture. Top with remaining cookie crumbs and whipped cream. Serve immediately.

Maple-Mocha Brownie Torte

PREP: 30 MIN. BAKE: 20 MIN. + COOLING MAKES: 12 SERVINGS

Ingredients

1 package brownie mix (13-in. x 9-in. pan size)
1/2 cup chopped walnuts
2 cups heavy whipping cream
2 teaspoons instant coffee granules
1/2 cup packed brown sugar 1
1/2 teaspoons maple flavoring
1 teaspoon vanilla extract
Chocolate curls or additional walnuts, optional

1. Prepare batter for brownie mix according to package directions for cake-like brownies. Stir in walnuts. Pour into two greased 9-in. round baking pans.
2. Bake at 350° for 20-22 minutes or until a toothpick inserted 2 in. from the edge comes out clean. Cool for 10 minutes before removing from pans to wire racks to cool completely.
3. In a large bowl, beat cream and coffee granules until stiff peaks form. Gradually beat in the brown sugar, maple flavoring and vanilla.
4. Spread 1 1/2 cups over one brownie layer; top with second layer. Spread remaining cream mixture over top and sides of torte. Garnish with chocolate curls or walnuts if desired. Store in the refrigerator.

Snowflake Pudding

PREP: 20 MIN. + CHILLING MAKES: 6 SERVINGS

Ingredients

1 envelope unflavored gelatin
1 1/4 cups cold 2% milk, divided
1/2 cup sugar
1/2 teaspoon salt
1 teaspoon vanilla extract
1 1/3 cups flaked coconut, toasted
1 cup heavy whipping cream, whipped

SAUCE

1 package (10 ounces) frozen sweetened raspberries, thawed
1 1/2 teaspoons cornstarch
1/2 cup red currant jelly

1. In a small saucepan, sprinkle gelatin over 1/4 cup milk; let stand for 1 minute. Heat over low heat, stirring until gelatin is completely dissolved.

2. In a large saucepan, combine the sugar, salt and remaining milk; heat just until sugar is dissolved. Remove from the heat; stir in gelatin mixture and vanilla. Refrigerate until partially set. Fold in coconut and whipped cream. Pour into dessert dishes; refrigerate for at least 2 hours.

3. Meanwhile, strain raspberries to remove seeds. In a small saucepan, combine the cornstarch, raspberry pulp and currant jelly; stir until smooth. Bring to a boil; cook and stir for 2 minutes or until thickened. Chill for at least 1 hour. Serve with pudding.

Coconut Angel Squares

PREP: 15 MIN. + CHILLING MAKES: 12-15 SERVINGS

Ingredients

1 prepared angel food cake (8 to 10 ounces), cut into 1/2-inch cubes
1 1/2 cups cold 2% milk
1 teaspoon coconut extract
2 packages (3.4 ounces each) instant vanilla pudding mix
1 quart vanilla ice cream, softened
1 cup flaked coconut, divided
1 carton (8 ounces) frozen whipped topping, thawed

1. Place cake cubes in a greased 13-in. x 9-in. dish. In a large bowl, whisk the milk, extract and pudding mixes for 2 minutes (mixture will be thick). Add ice cream and 3/4 cup coconut; beat on low just until combined.
2. Spoon over cake cubes. Spread with whipped topping. Toast remaining coconut; sprinkle over top. Cover and chill for at least 1 hour. Refrigerate leftovers.

Pomegranate Poached Pears

PREP: 20 MIN. COOK: 1 HOUR 25 MIN. MAKES: 6 SERVINGS

Ingredients

3 cups dry red wine or red grape juice
1 bottle (16 ounces) pomegranate juice
1 cup water
1/2 cup sugar
1/4 cup orange juice
2 tablespoons grated orange peel
3 fresh rosemary sprigs (4 inches)
1 cinnamon stick (3 inches)
6 medium pears
6 orange slices
6 tablespoons Mascarpone cheese

1. In a Dutch oven, combine the first eight ingredients. Core pears from the bottom, leaving stems intact. Peel pears; place on their sides in the pan. Bring to a boil. Reduce heat; cover and simmer for 25-30 minutes or until pears are almost tender. Remove with a slotted spoon; cool.

2. Strain poaching liquid and return to Dutch oven. Bring to a boil; cook until reduced to 1 cup, about 45 minutes. Discard rosemary and cinnamon. Place an orange slice on each serving plate; top with 1 tablespoon cheese and a pear. Drizzle with poaching liquid.

Berries with Champagne Cream

PREP: 20 MIN. + CHILLING MAKES: 6 SERVINGS

Ingredients

8 egg yolks
1/2 cup sugar
1 cup champagne
1 cup heavy whipping cream, whipped
1 pint fresh raspberries
1 pint fresh strawberries

1. In a heavy saucepan, beat egg yolks and sugar with a portable mixer until thick and lemon-colored. Gradually beat in champagne. Place the saucepan over low heat. With a portable mixer, beat on low speed for 1 minute. Continue beating over low heat until mixture reaches 160°, about 5-6 minutes.
2. Cool quickly by placing pan in bowl of ice water; stir for 2 minutes. Press plastic wrap onto surface of custard. Refrigerate to chill.
3. Fold in whipped cream. Spoon three-quarters of the champagne cream into stemmed glasses. Top with berries. Spoon remaining champagne cream over berries.

Raspberry Fondue Dip

PREP/TOTAL TIME: 25 MIN. MAKES: ABOUT 1 CUP

Ingredients

1 package (10 ounces) frozen sweetened raspberries
1 cup apple butter
1 tablespoon Red Hots candies
2 teaspoons cornstarch
Assorted fresh fruit

1. Thaw and drain raspberries, reserving 1 tablespoon juice. Mash raspberries. Press through a fine- mesh strainer into a small saucepan; discard seeds.
2. Add apple butter and Red Hots to strained raspberries; cook over medium heat until candies are dissolved, stirring occasionally. Combine cornstarch and reserved juice until smooth; stir into berry mixture. Bring to a boil; cook and stir over medium heat for 1-2 minutes or until thickened.
3. To serve warm, transfer to a small fondue pot and keep warm. Or, to serve cold, refrigerate until chilled. Serve with fruit.

Steamed Cranberry-Molasses Pudding

PREP: 15 MIN. COOK: 1 HOUR MAKES: 8-10 SERVINGS

Ingredients

1 1/3 cups all-purpose flour
2 teaspoons baking soda
1 teaspoon baking powder
1/2 cup molasses
1/3 cup hot water
2 cups chopped fresh or frozen cranberries
BUTTER SAUCE
1/2 cup butter, cubed
1 cup sugar
1 cup heavy whipping cream

1. In a large bowl, combine the flour, baking soda and baking powder. Combine molasses and water; stir into dry ingredients. Fold in cranberries. Pour into a well-greased 4-cup pudding mold; cover.
2. Place mold on a rack in a deep stockpot; add 1 in. of hot water to pan. Bring to a gentle boil; cover and steam for 1 hour or until a toothpick inserted near the center comes out clean, adding water to pan as needed. Let stand for 5 minutes before removing from mold.
3. In a small saucepan, melt butter; stir in sugar and cream. Cook and stir over medium heat for 3-5 minutes or until heated through. Unmold pudding onto a serving plate; cut into wedges. Serve warm with sauce.

Candy Sampler

Chocolate-Coated Pretzels

PREP: 15 MIN. + STANDING MAKES: 5-6 DOZEN

Ingredients

1 to 1 1/4 pounds white and/or milk chocolate candy coating, coarsely chopped
1 package (8 ounces) miniature pretzels
Nonpariels, colored jimmies and colored sugar, optional

In a microwave, melt half of candy coating at a time; stir until smooth. Dip pretzels in candy coating; allow excess to drip off. Place on waxed paper; let stand until almost set. Garnish as desired; let stand until set.

Cookie Dough Truffles

PREP: 1 HOUR + CHILLING MAKES: 5 1/2 DOZEN

Ingredients

1/2 cup butter, softened
3/4 cup packed brown sugar
1 teaspoon vanilla extract
2 cups all-purpose flour
1 can (14 ounces) sweetened condensed milk
1/2 cup miniature semisweet chocolate chips
1/2 cup chopped walnuts
1 1/2 pounds dark chocolate candy coating, coarsely chopped

1. In a large bowl, cream the butter and brown sugar until light and fluffy. Beat in vanilla. Gradually add flour alternately with milk, beating well after each addition. Stir in chocolate chips and walnuts.
2. Shape into 1-in. balls; place on waxed paper-lined baking sheets. Loosely cover and refrigerate for 1-2 hours or until firm.
3. In microwave, melt candy coating; stir until smooth. Dip balls in coating; allow excess to drip off. Place on waxed paper-lined baking sheets. Refrigerate until firm, about 15 min. If desired, remelt remaining candy coating and drizzle over candies. Store in the refrigerator.

Butterscotch Fudge

PREP/TOTAL TIME: 25 MIN. MAKES: ABOUT 1 1/2 POUNDS

Ingredients

1 teaspoon plus 2 tablespoons butter, divided
1 2/3 cups sugar
2/3 cup evaporated milk
1/2 teaspoon salt
2 cups miniature marshmallows
1 package (10 to 11 ounces) butterscotch chips
1/2 cup chopped walnuts
1 teaspoon maple flavoring

1. Line an 8-in. square pan with foil and grease the foil with 1 teaspoon butter; set aside.
2. In a large saucepan, combine the sugar, milk, salt and remaining butter; cook and stir over medium heat until mixture comes to a boil. Boil for 5 minutes, stirring constantly.
3. Remove from the heat; add the marshmallows, chips, nuts and maple flavoring. Stir until marshmallows and chips are melted. Spoon into prepared pan. Let stand until set.
4. Using foil, lift fudge out of pan. Discard foil; cut fudge into 1-in squares. Store in an airtight container at room temperature.

Raisin Cashew Drops

PREP: 20 MIN. + CHILLING MAKES: 2 1/2 POUNDS

Ingredients

2 cups (12 ounces) semisweet chocolate chips
1 can (14 ounces) sweetened condensed milk
1 tablespoon light corn syrup
1 teaspoon vanilla extract
2 cups coarsely chopped cashews
2 cups raisins

1. In a heavy saucepan over low heat, melt chocolate chips with milk and corn syrup for 10-12 minutes, stirring occasionally. Remove from the heat; stir in vanilla until blended. Stir in cashews and raisins.
2. Drop by teaspoonfuls onto waxed paper-lined baking sheets. Refrigerate for 3 hours or until firm. Store in the refrigerator.

So-Easy Truffles

PREP: 45 MIN. MAKES: 4 DOZEN

Ingredients

1 package (15 1/2 ounces) Oreo cookies
1 package (8 ounces) cream cheese, cubed
1 cup chocolate wafer crumbs

Place cookies in a food processor; cover and process until finely crushed. Add cream cheese; process until blended. Roll into 1-in. balls. Roll in wafer crumbs. Store in an airtight container in the refrigerator.

Peanut Butter Truffles: *Substitute a 16-oz. package of peanut butter cream-filled sandwich cookies for the chocolate sandwich cookies. Omit chocolate wafer crumbs. Melt 12 ounces of milk chocolate candy coating; stir until smooth. Dip balls in chocolate; place on waxed paper until set. Store in the refrigerator. Makes: 4 dozen.*

Vanilla Cookie Truffles: *Substitute a 16-oz. package of cream-filled vanilla sandwich cookies for the chocolate sandwich cookies. Melt 12 ounces of milk chocolate candy coating; stir until smooth. Dip balls in chocolate; sprinkle with 1/4 cup chocolate crumbs. Place on waxed paper until set. Store in the refrigerator.Makes: 4 dozen.*

Snowball

PREP: 20 MIN. + FREEZING MAKES: ABOUT 3 DOZEN

Ingredients

1/2 cup butter, cubed
1 can (14 ounces) sweetened condensed milk
3 tablespoons baking cocoa
1 teaspoon vanilla extract
2 cups graham cracker crumbs (about 32 squares)
3 1/2 cups flaked coconut, divided
32 to 35 large marshmallows

1. Line a baking sheet with waxed paper; set aside.
2. In a large saucepan, combine the butter, milk, cocoa and vanilla. Cook and stir over medium heat until butter is melted and mixture is smooth. Remove from the heat; stir in cracker crumbs and 1 1/2 cups coconut. Let stand until cool enough to handle.
3. Using moistened hands, wrap about 1 tablespoon of mixture around each marshmallow (dip hands in water often to prevent sticking). Roll in remaining coconut; place on prepared baking sheet. Cover and freeze until firm. Store in an airtight container in the refrigerator or freezer. May be frozen for up to 2 months.

Cinnamon Walnut Brittle

PREP: 20 MIN. + COOLING MAKES: 3/4 POUND

Ingredients

1 cup sugar
1/2 cup light corn syrup
1 cup chopped walnuts
1 teaspoon butter
1/2 teaspoon ground cinnamon
1 teaspoon baking soda
1 teaspoon vanilla extract

1. Butter a baking sheet; set aside. In a 2-qt. microwave-safe bowl, combine sugar and corn syrup. Microwave, uncovered, on high for 3 minutes; stir. Cook, uncovered, on high 2 1/2 minutes longer. Stir in the walnuts, butter and cinnamon.
2. Microwave, uncovered, on high for 2 minutes longer or until mixture turns a light amber color (mixture will be very hot).
3. Quickly stir in baking soda and vanilla until light and foamy. Immediately pour onto prepared pan; spread with a metal spatula. Cool; break into pieces.

Editor's Note: *This recipe was tested in a 1,100-watt microwave.*

Toasted Coconut Truffles

PREP: 30 MIN. + CHILLING MAKES: ABOUT 5 1/2 DOZEN

Ingredients

4 cups (24 ounces) semisweet chocolate chips
1 package (8 ounces) cream cheese, softened and cubed
3/4 cup sweetened condensed milk
3 teaspoons vanilla extract
2 teaspoons water
1 pound white candy coating, coarsely chopped
2 tablespoons flaked coconut, finely chopped and toasted

1. In a microwave-safe bowl, melt chocolate chips; stir until smooth. Add the cream cheese, milk, vanilla and water; beat with a hand mixer until blended. Cover and refrigerate until easy to handle, about 1 1/2 hours.
2. Shape into 1-in. balls and place on waxed paper-lined baking sheets. Loosely cover and refrigerate for 1-2 hours or until firm.
3. In a microwave, melt candy coating, stir until smooth. Dip balls in coating; allow excess to drip off. Place on waxed paper-lined baking sheets. Sprinkle with coconut. Refrigerate until firm, about 15 minutes. Store in the refrigerator in an airtight container.

Holiday Divinity

PREP: 25 MIN. COOK: 15 MIN. MAKES: 1 1/4 POUNDS

Ingredients

2 cups sugar
1/2 cup water
1/3 cup light corn syrup
2 egg whites
1 teaspoon vanilla extract
1/8 teaspoon salt
1 cup chopped walnuts, toasted
1/4 cup diced candied cherries
1/4 cup diced candied pineapple

1. In a heavy saucepan, combine the sugar, water and corn syrup; cook and stir until sugar is dissolved and mixture comes to a boil. Cook over medium heat, without stirring, until a candy thermometer reads 250° (hard-ball stage). Remove from the heat.
2. Meanwhile, in a stand mixer, beat the egg whites until stiff peaks form. With mixer running on high speed, carefully pour hot syrup in a slow, steady stream into the mixing bowl. Add vanilla and salt. Beat on high speed just until candy loses its gloss and holds its shape, about 10 minutes. Stir in nuts and fruit.
3. Drop by teaspoonfuls onto waxed paper. Store in airtight containers. **Editor's Note:** *The use of a hand mixer is not recommended for this recipe.*

Peanut Butter Chocolate Cups

PREP: 20 MIN. + CHILLING MAKES: 1 DOZEN

Ingredients

1 milk chocolate candy bar (7 ounces)
1/4 cup butter
1 tablespoon shortening
1/4 cup creamy peanut butter

1. In a microwave, melt the chocolate, butter and shortening; stir until smooth. Place foil or paper miniature baking cups in a miniature muffin tin. Place 1 tablespoon of chocolate mixture in each cup.
2. In a microwave, melt peanut butter; stir until smooth. Spoon into cups. Top with remaining chocolate mixture. Remelt chocolate mixture if necessary. Refrigerate for 30 minutes or until firm.

117

Thank you!

For purchasing this book. Your order made our day! We hope we make yours
If you have any questions about this book, contact us anytime. We'd love to hear from you. Are you happy with your book?

Yes 😊   No ☹

Great! Than please share your review online

Please contact us at roxiebrads@yahoo.com

CPSIA information can be obtained
at www.ICGtesting.com
Printed in the USA
BVHW011634021221
623087BV00002B/5